TOUCHSTONES OF DESIGN
[re]defining public architecture

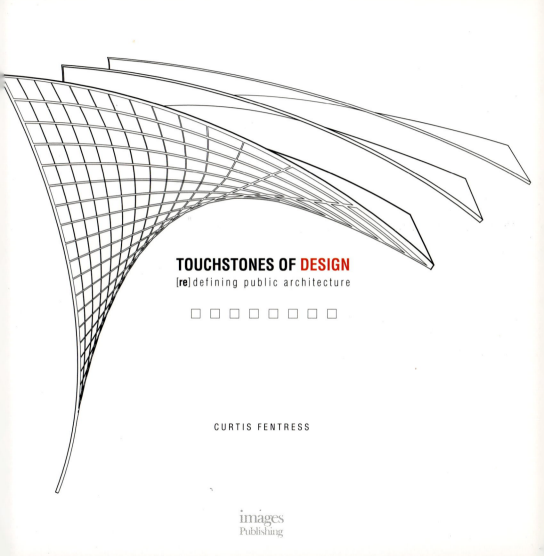

TOUCHSTONES OF DESIGN
[re]defining public architecture

CURTIS FENTRESS

images
Publishing

Published in Australia in 2010 by
The Images Publishing Group Pty Ltd
ABN 89 059 734 431
6 Bastow Place, Mulgrave, Victoria 3170, Australia
Tel: +61 3 9561 5544 Fax: +61 3 9561 4860
books@imagespublishing.com
www.imagespublishing.com

Copyright © The Images Publishing Group Pty Ltd 2010
The Images Publishing Group Reference Number: 898 (Standard format edition)
The Images Publishing Group Reference Number: 901 (Small format edition)

All rights reserved. Apart from any fair dealing for the purposes of
private study, research, criticism or review as permitted under the
Copyright Act, no part of this publication may be reproduced, stored in
a retrieval system or transmitted in any form by any means, electronic,
mechanical, photocopying, recording or otherwise, without the written
permission of the publisher.

Other publications on Curtis Fentress or the Fentress studio:

Portal to the Corps | 2007
National Museum of the Marine Corps | Curtis Worth Fentress | 2006
10 Airports | 2006
Museums + Theaters | 2003
Civic Builders | Curtis W. Fentress | 2002
Architecture in the Public Interest | 2001
Fentress Bradburn Architects | 2001
Gateway to the West: Denver International Airport | Jessica Sommers | 2000
Master Architect Series III | 1998
Fentress Bradburn Architects | Roger A. Chandler | 1995
Curtis Worth Fentress | 1995

National Library of Australia Cataloguing-in-Publication entry

Author:	Fentress, Curtis.
Title:	Touchstones of design: redefining public architecture / Curtis Fentress.
ISBN:	9781864703825 (hbk standard format edition)
	9781864704013 (hbk small format edition)
Subjects:	Fentress Architects.
	Public architecture.
	Public architecture—Philosophy.
	Architectural design—Philosophy.
Dewey Number:	720.103

Coordinating editors: Agatha Kessler, Mary Voelz Chandler

Designed by: Agatha Kessler, Curtis Fentress, Dylan McQuinn, Jason Knowles, Matthew Breest

Cover photograph by: Ron Johnson

Pre-publishing services by Chroma Graphics (Overseas) Pte Ltd, Singapore

Printed on 150 gsm Quatro Silk Matt paper by Everbest Printing Co. Ltd., in Hong Kong/China

IMAGES has included on its website a page for special notices in relation to this and our other publications. Please visit www.imagespublishing.com.

The American Institute of Architects has honored Curtis Fentress with the 2010 Thomas Jefferson Award for Public Architecture, which recognizes one architect in the public sector with a portfolio of accomplishments that evidences great depth while making a significant contribution to the quality of public architecture.

CONTENTS

to **BEGIN**

with **THANKS**

FOREWORD

THE TOUCHSTONES OF DESIGN

1. discover the natural order
2. use context to create identity
3. let culture guide design
4. celebrate the entry
5. listen closely
6. stay focused
7. restrain the ego
 design for people

BIOGRAPHY

TEAM

NUMBERS

CREDITS

TIMELINE

I've always loved to draw. My early drawings of airplanes were on the walls of a tiny two-room log cabin – my first home. Reading was a challenge, but drawing was a release. Pictures called to me louder than words.

That love of drawing led me into architecture. With the encouragement of my art and drafting teachers in high school, I worked hard to get into college, where I pursued the field of design and architecture.

My desire to be an architect was to make the built environment a better place and hopefully to make peoples' lives better. Large-scale public projects seemed to be the greatest challenge. But they also could have the biggest impact on a community.

After earning a professional bachelor's degree in architecture from North Carolina State University's College of Design, I went to New York. There I continued my studies of architecture, taking classes at Columbia University in the evenings and working for I.M. Pei and Kohn Pedersen Fox before starting a practice in Denver in 1980.

Throughout the years, many people have been instrumental in our work. I have been grateful to learn from clients, communities and associates, as well as the many talented people who have been members of our studio. During these decades of creating public projects, I adopted and still follow a design philosophy I call the Touchstones of Design.

While these Touchstones are not earth-shattering, like kindness and integrity, they provide guidance, forming a foundation and principles for my approach to design. They sound simple. And yet, these ideals are difficult both to identify and achieve. The same is true in the professional arena, where the approach to design requires honesty and commitment.

The Touchstones speak to two themes central to my work. The first is the balance of creativity and discipline. That's where the first seven Touchstones come into play. They talk about a process of discovery. They make peoples' needs and wants integral to a design. It has been gratifying to see communities respond, watching how a building influences their lives. Past and present meet here, in public architecture that is a mix of function and art.

The final Touchstone on designing in the arena of public architecture is all about people – now, and for generations to come. It addresses the second theme – respect for people, their environment and the role of the conscientious architect. It talks about the future. A design is often literally set in stone through a huge orchestrated effort of many different professions. This is a humbling process, one that demands that you push beyond physical constraints to find the infinite, the place where timeless design elevates and restores. It's a leap, often without a safety net, that every architect is obliged to take.

I offer these Touchstones of Design, not as industry best practices, but simply as sources from which I have drawn my own insights. In one sense, architecture performs a service for people. It also fuels the drive toward timeless design. But ultimately, architecture means picking up the pencil every morning to design the best building you can for the people who will experience it.

FORTY YEARS IS JUST THE BEGINNING.

with **THANKS**

Touchstones of Design: [re]defining public architecture is being released just in time to celebrate 30 years of design by Fentress Architects. Although the studio is no stranger to creating a book, with each new publication we find parallels to the challenges and satisfaction presented by the design and construction of a building. And as buildings last, so do books.

Our design studio would not exist without the incredible clients who have believed in us. That holds true, too, with the countless individuals who have been part of this team, demonstrating their commitment and shared belief in the importance of public architecture.

That's the key difference with the field we have pursued. Public architecture is designed by people, for people. And each project is an act of collective engagement, where the talents, energy and determination of many people come together.

The same is true with this book. To make it happen, numerous people worked tirelessly and creatively, and with much laughter. I'd like to say that this person did this and that person did that, but that was not the case. Everyone pulled together, meeting in the evenings after our day jobs to pursue something we all believe in. We were joined by a small Scottie dog named Clover, who entertained us along the way with her constant games of fetch. She helped us keep a sense of humor long into the nights.

The core team brought to reality a book that is part diary, part revelation through images and sketches found in our archives, and part lesson in who we are, what we do, and why we do it. The pages of this book illustrate my design philosophy and approach to the art of public architecture, as captured in time by Agatha Kessler, Jason Knowles, Matt Breest, Dylan McQuinn, Mary Voelz Chandler, Matthew Popowski and Jennifer Ito. Images Publishing also believes in us and has published several prior books about the studio. They are consummate professionals. Their Australian humor has made many evenings fun.

TO ALL, I CANNOT THANK YOU **ENOUGH.**

FOREWORD

The architect's monograph has become a well-worn path. It is typically a published piece that is an extension of a not very well veiled marketing plan. For some it has become an opportunity to tell the stories of projects in the most favorable light with the most erudite insights. Such publications become extensions of the ego of the individual without really revealing the fundamental value system of either the individual or the office team responsible for the work.

What Curt Fentress has produced is quite different. This is a work that begins with the underlying values of an individual demonstrating the connection between what is believed and what is made. It is an intimate conversation that has the feeling of the kind of discussion that architects have when they drift into thoughts about why they ever embarked on their professional journeys. It is an expression of the importance of the team and a sincere appreciation for the value of a great client. It is about relationships and the patient interwoven search that defines them in the creation of architecture. There is a genuine sense of discovery, enthusiasm and joy about the book. This spirit is reflected in the great halls of airports clearly building on the legacy of the great train stations. It is about the passion for organizing ideas that guide architecture from the incredible expression of the National Museum of the Marine Corps to the iconic tent structures of Denver International Airport representing the most nomadic culture of all, modern flight.

There is a real, true feeling to this work. Perhaps it is the sense of respect for the deepest values such as a mature relationship to the land as it is expressed in the National Museum of Wildlife Art. Perhaps it is in the first sentences of the monograph that link personal, private really, weaknesses and strengths. It is no surprise that visual images and drawing are the vocabulary of this architect and his team. This is a publication filled with provocative, stimulating images. It brings to mind the wonderful book *Thinking in Pictures* by Temple Grandin. It is clear that Curt Fentress and his closest collaborators subscribe to this notion as a way to proceed with the conceptualization of architecture; there is no other way to understand this work.

I encourage all who have a passion for architecture and wonder if the practice of this discipline has retained its intimate character to spend time with this book. It will cause you to experience Mr. Fentress very deeply.

Marvin J. Malecha *FAIA*
2009 President of the American Institute of Architects
Dean, North Carolina State University College of Design

01

Process
Purpose
Discovery
Immersion
Confluence

DISCOVER THE **NATURAL ORDER**

Public buildings involve process and commitment, periods of reflection and flashes of illumination.

This process of discovery requires a psychological immersion in the realms of client, community and site, creating the potential for a timeless design.

As people move through a building, they help shape it. It's a natural flow, as people become one with architecture.

NATURAL ORDER

FEED CONVEYORS FOR

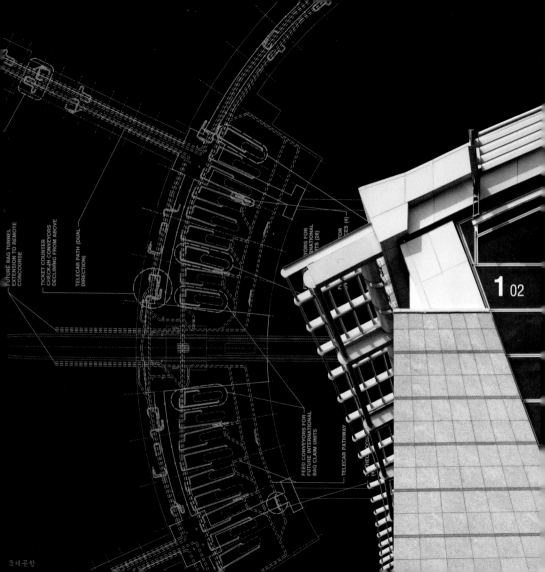

NATURAL ORDER

I don't begin with a preconceived notion of what a building should be.
It is not a sculpture.

I prefer to patiently search through extensive discovery until I find a
seam somewhere, crack it open and...

DISCOVER THE ART INSIDE.

NATURAL ORDER

1 04

NATURAL ORDER

PROCESS

PURPOSE

DISCOVERY

IMMERSION

CONFLUENCE

1.05

NATURAL ORDER

1.06

NATURAL ORDER

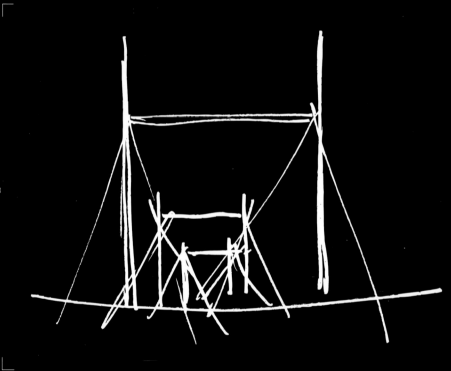

1.07

NATURAL ORDER

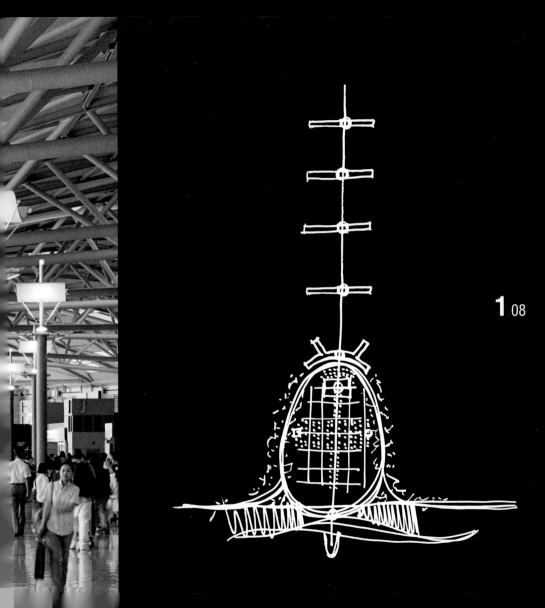

1.08

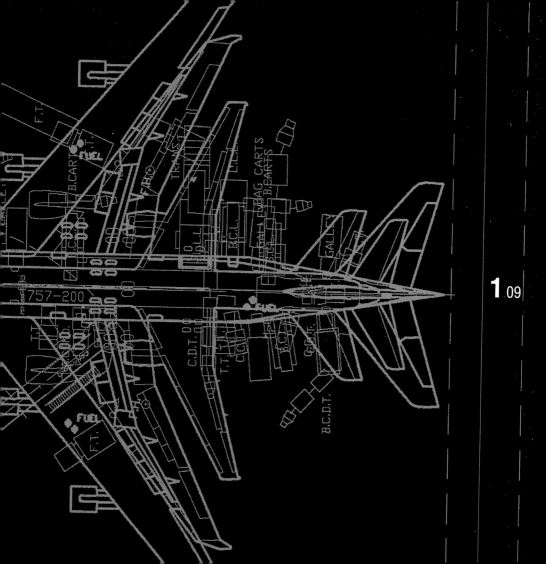

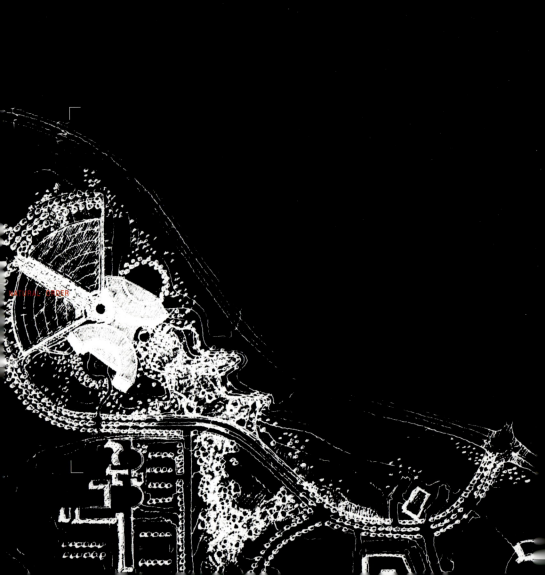

NATURAL ORDER

1.11

NATURAL ORDER

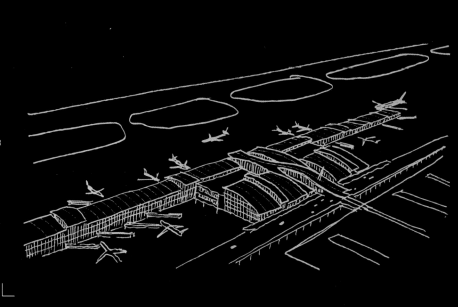

1.12

NATURAL ORDER

1.14

NATURAL ORDER

To question, to reason, are essential parts of the CREATIVE PROCESS.
Rationality unearths the irrational "AHA" moments.

1.15

DISCOVER THE NATURAL ORDER

USE CONTEXT TO CREATE AN IDENTITY

LET CULTURE GUIDE DESIGN

CELEBRATE THE ENTRY

1 16

LISTEN CLOSELY

STAY FOCUSED

RESTRAIN THE EGO

DESIGN FOR PEOPLE

0₂

- Place
- History
- The Senses
- Symbolism
- Humanism

USE CONTEXT TO **CREATE IDENTITY**

Context is more than an intellectual consideration of the history or physical appearance of a neighborhood, city, or state, and it's more than the way new will live with old. Context also draws on the senses, the sights, the smells, and the memories that define a place and make it unique. Context grows from community, and people respond to it.

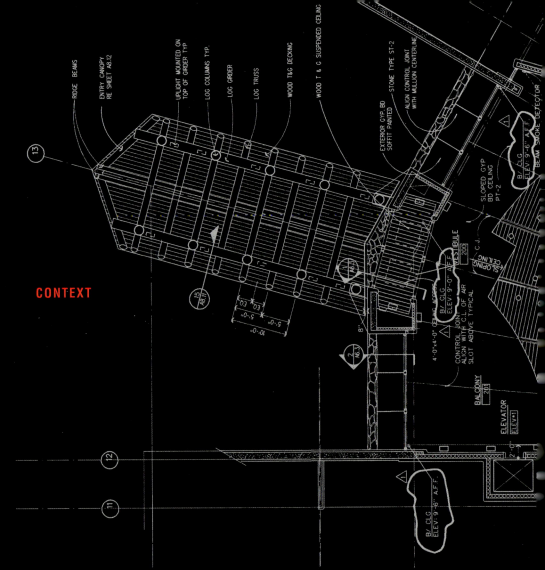
CONTEXT

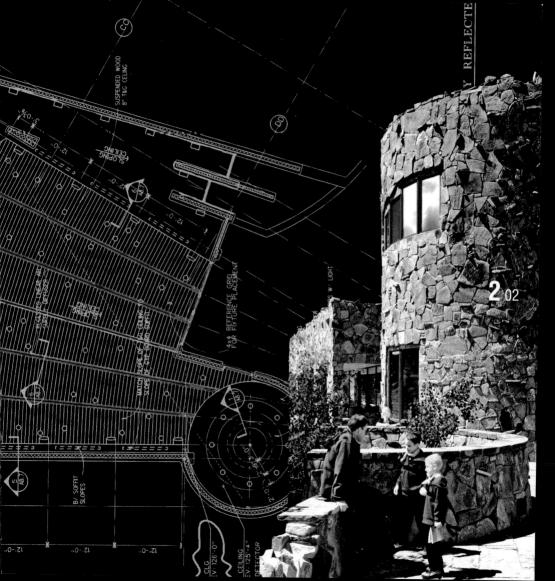

CONTEXT

Icons emerge from context. It could be a historic moment like the Marines at Iwo Jima; a natural endowment like the Rocky Mountains; a feeling of survival as I looked at plants struggling for water on the desert floor; or native crafts in Korean huts with thatched roofs... the pragmatic is just waiting to BECOME DRAMATIC.

2 03

We try not to start with concepts. It's physical. We walk and study the site. Use all the senses. We immerse ourselves in research, getting our heads in the culture. What stands out? I don't mean the obvious — don't make the building look like an iconic cactus. Look at the story — plants struggling to live in that environment. What colors, shapes, texture, movement, drama need to be in the story of your building?

2.04

CONTEXT

2.05

CONTEXT

CONTEXT IS EVERYWHERE...
you have to see what parts speak up.

2.06

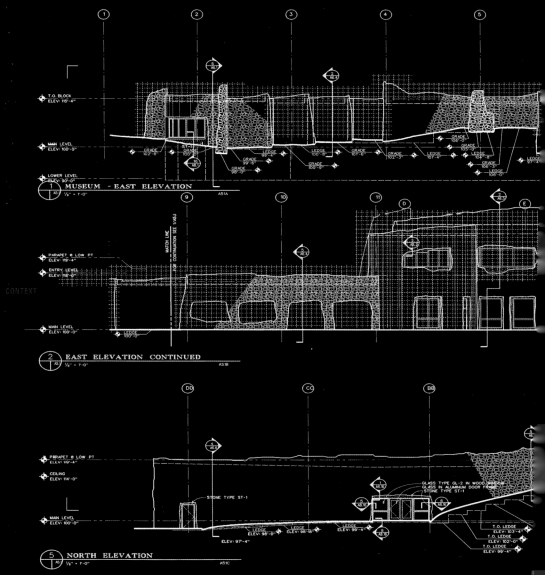

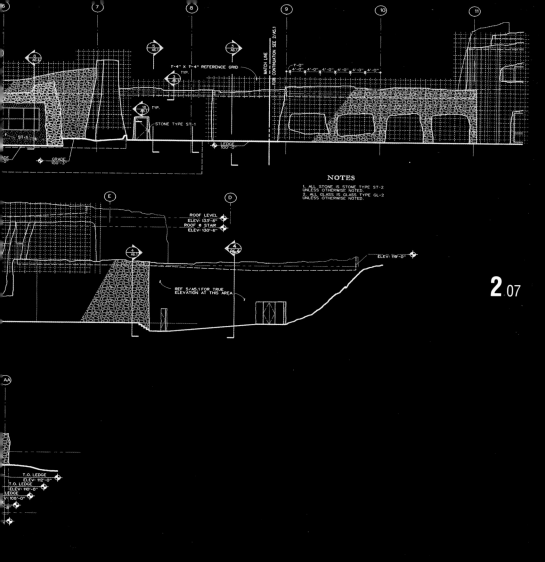

2.08

CONTEXT

CONTEXT

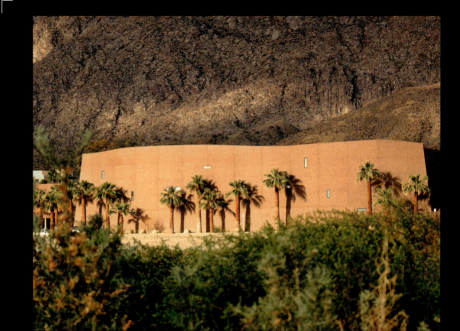

2.10

CONTEXT

PLACE

HISTORY

THE SENSES

SYMBOLISM

HUMANISM

2.11

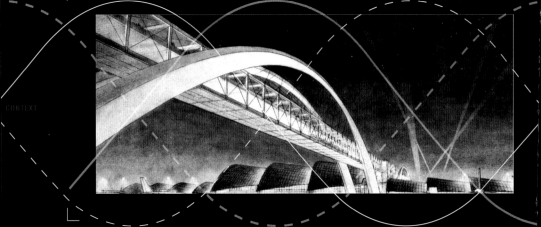

CONTEXT

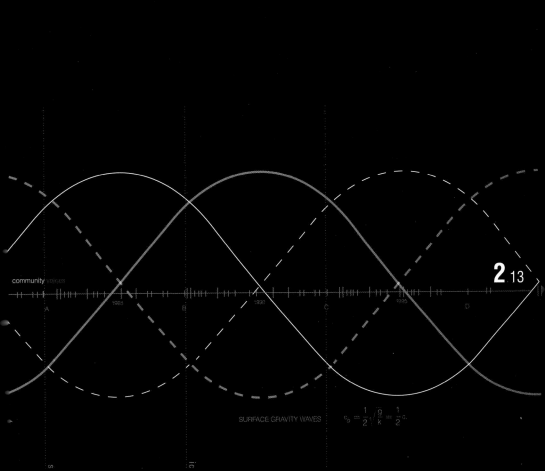

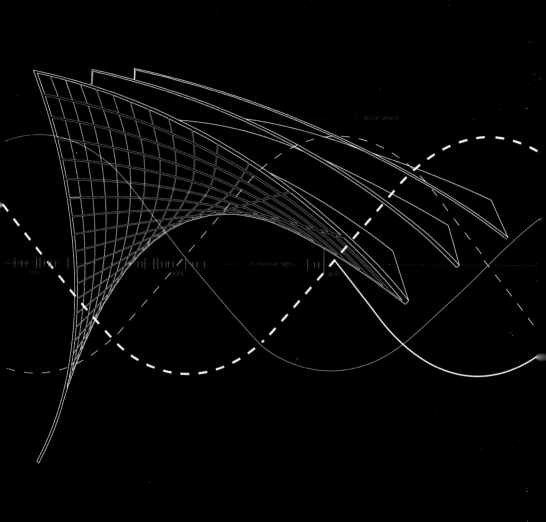

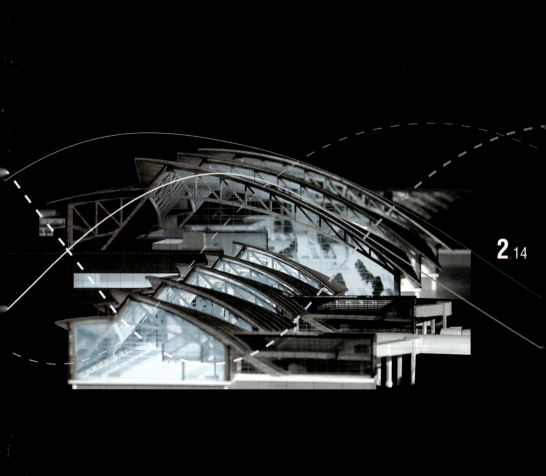

2.14

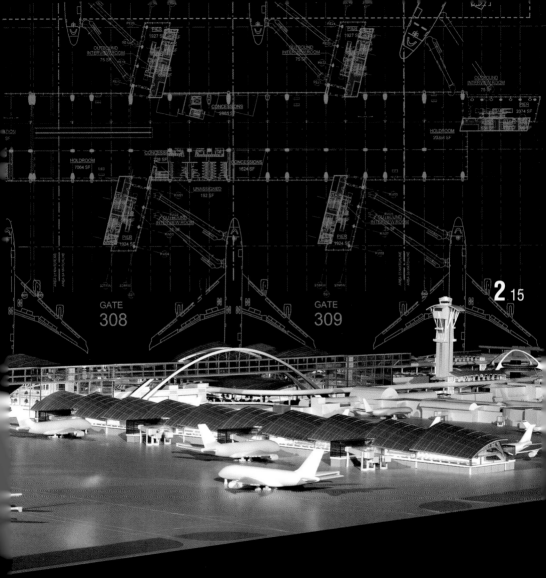

CONTEXT

DISCOVER THE NATURAL ORDER

LET CULTURE GUIDE DESIGN

CELEBRATE THE ENTRY

2.16

LISTEN CLOSELY

STAY FOCUSED

RESTRAIN THE EGO

DESIGN FOR PEOPLE

0₃

> Flow
> Pride
> Respect
> Tradition
> Community

LET CULTURE GUIDE DESIGN

The collective beliefs, traditions and aspirations of a society — culture — help define and influence how individuals live. And experience has shown that incorporating cultural references in design has a powerful effect on the ability to attract and unify.

It is a power I strive to harness, especially since our work takes us to places as distinct as the deserts of the Middle East, the lofty peaks of the West and the vibrant cities of Asia.

Whether the project is a museum, airport or convention center, national and regional influences help shape design and the choice of materials.

Civic buildings capture and reflect the shared strengths of a community, reinforcing pride in residents as well as stirring curiosity and respect in visitors.

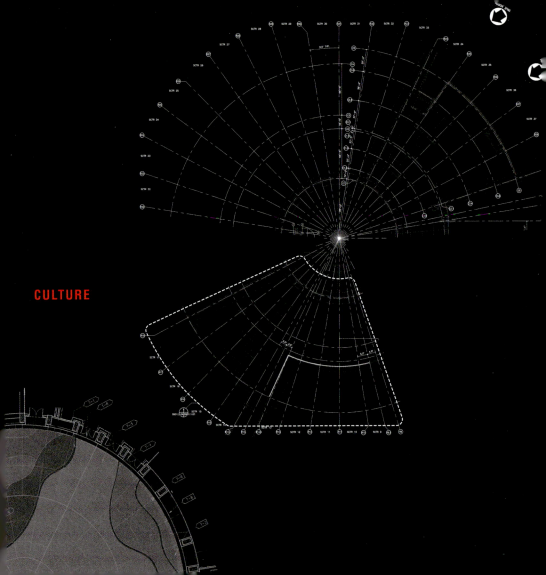

CULTURE

CULTURE

There are many satisfactions in public architecture, but one of the greatest is the moment when you unveil a project and suddenly a group of adults — stakeholders, public officials — forget themselves and light up like kids dancing around the model, pointing and saying,

3.03

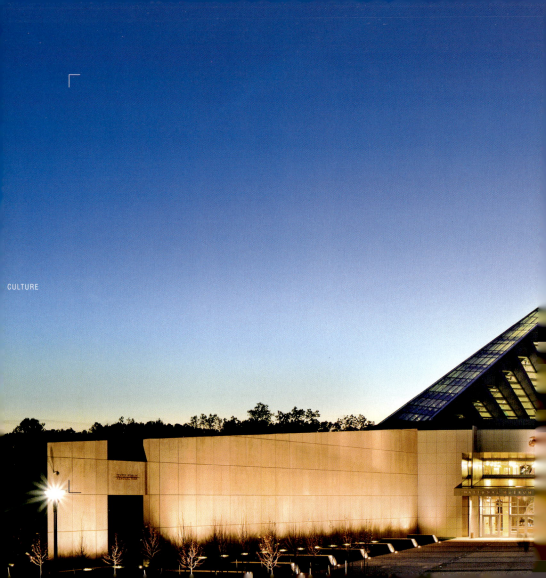

CULTURE

3.04

FLOW

PRIDE

RESPECT

TRADITION

COMMUNITY

CULTURE

3.05

CULTURE

3.06

CULTURE

3.09

FLOW

PRIDE

RESPECT

TRADITION

COMMUNITY

CULTURE

3.11

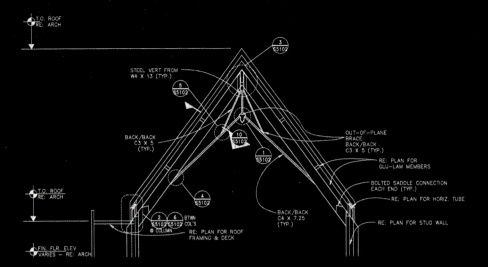

Iconic architecture has come to mean many things... not all of them good.

To me, iconic simply means that the building stands for **SOMETHING OF VALUE** to the people for whom it was built.

MY GOAL IS NOT TO EXPLAIN, BUT TO SUGGEST THE ESSENCE.　　　**3**.14

CULTURE

3.15

LET CULTURE GUIDE DESIGN

DISCOVER THE NATURAL ORDER

USE CONTEXT TO CREATE AN IDENTITY

CELEBRATE THE ENTRY

LISTEN CLOSELY

STAY FOCUSED

RESTRAIN THE EGO

DESIGN FOR PEOPLE

3 16

04

[Unveil
Intuitive
Thoughtful
Welcoming
Practical Magic]

CELEBRATE THE ENTRY

A visitor's first encounter with a building — the approach — sets the tone for the experience within.

Buildings should welcome those who enter, offering a mix of drama and intuition and a chance to stop and reflect. Visitors know at a glance where to enter. Once inside, they find easy-to-read spaces that prompt the next step.

The sweep of the plaza leading to the National Museum of the Marine Corps beckons visitors to come in. The low-slung, circular Jefferson County Human Services Building encircles a visitor with open arms, a symbol of shelter to those in need.

Simplicity always trumps confusion.

ENTRY

There are many ways to celebrate the entrance of a building. In some situations there is the opportunity of a storybook opening.

You glimpse part of the structure from the highway like the beginning of a mystery unfolding. You wind toward the castle, getting a staccato view through the trees. As you approach you are surprised to be greeted by an archway that opens into a courtyard. This experience can be recreated with small portals that explode into a soaring overhead space.

Consider how THE BUILDING UNVEILS ITSELF to the user.

4 03

4 04

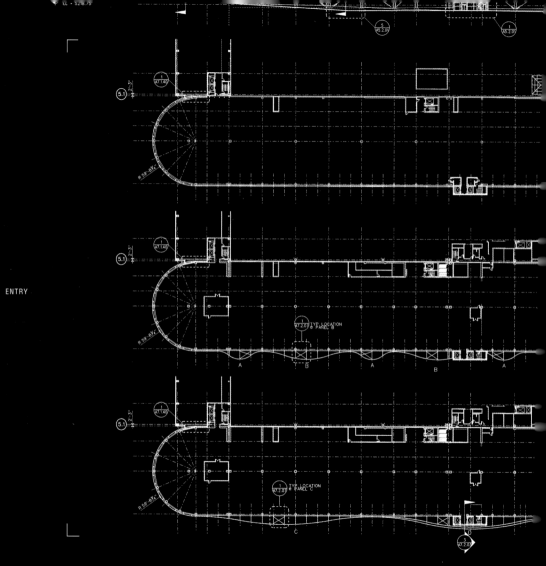
ENTRY

4.05

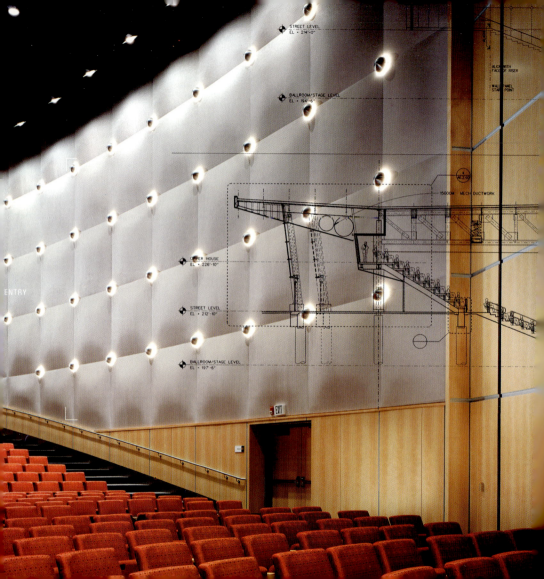

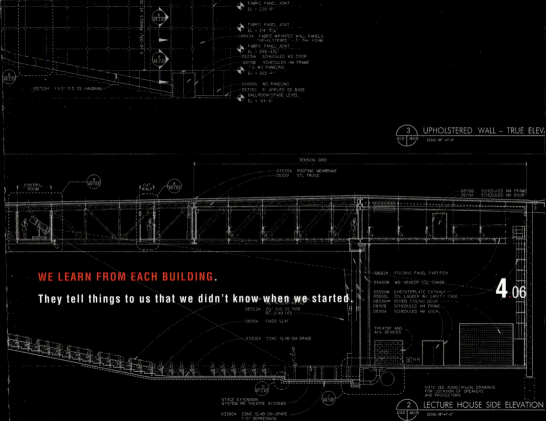

ENTRY

"Form follows function" – what does that mean? Does function take into account the full range of human needs – the need for safety, comfort, a sense of belonging, identity,

and the UPLIFTING OF THE SPIRIT through art.

4.07

ENTRY

UNVEIL

INTUITIVE

THOUGHTFUL

WELCOMING

PRACTICAL MAGIC

ENTRY

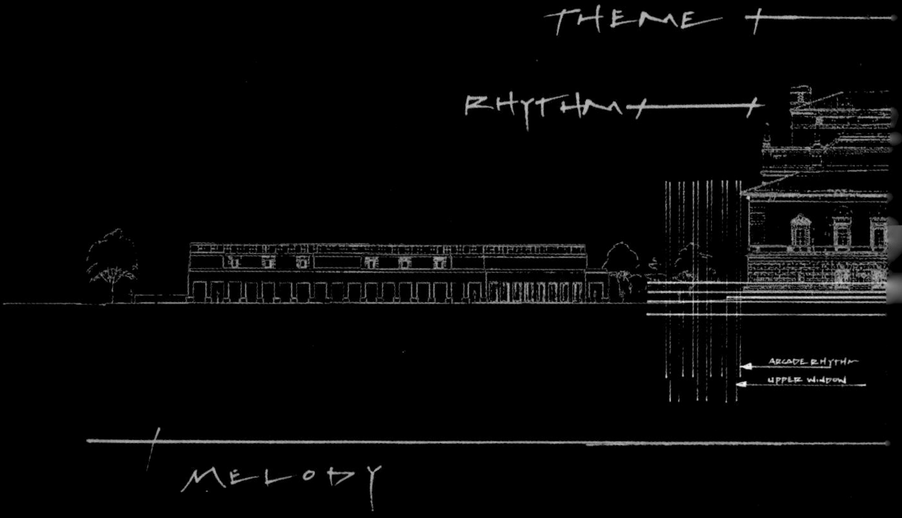

THEME
RHYTHM
ARCADE RHYTHM
UPPER WINDOW

MELODY

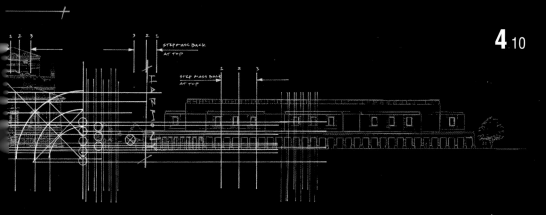

4.11

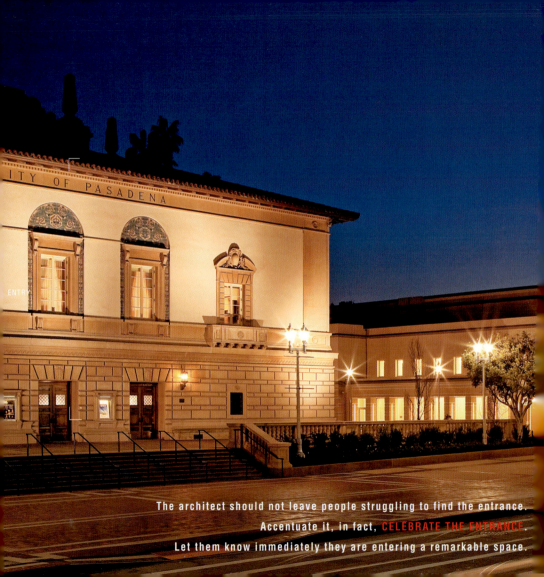

4.12

4.13

ENTRY

UNVEIL
INTUITIVE
THOUGHTFUL
WELCOMING

PRACTICAL MAGIC

4 14

CELEBRATE THE ENTRY

DISCOVER THE NATURAL ORDER

USE CONTEXT TO CREATE AN IDENTITY

LET CULTURE GUIDE DESIGN

LISTEN CLOSELY

STAY FOCUSED

RESTRAIN THE EGO

DESIGN FOR PEOPLE

4 16

05
LISTEN CLOSELY

- Unity
- Voices
- Receive
- Openness
- Commitment

The creation of great public architecture is a social act, uniting people and place in a complex and worthwhile pursuit.

The decision-maker is no longer a single owner or official. Instead, this vital role now belongs to the community. It is how a community gains a voice and a civic building becomes better. People give their time, their emotion, and their commitment in a personal act of community.

I welcome this process, because only then can a community problem be solved or a collective need met. I become a translator, using their vocabulary to design a timeless building for the common good.

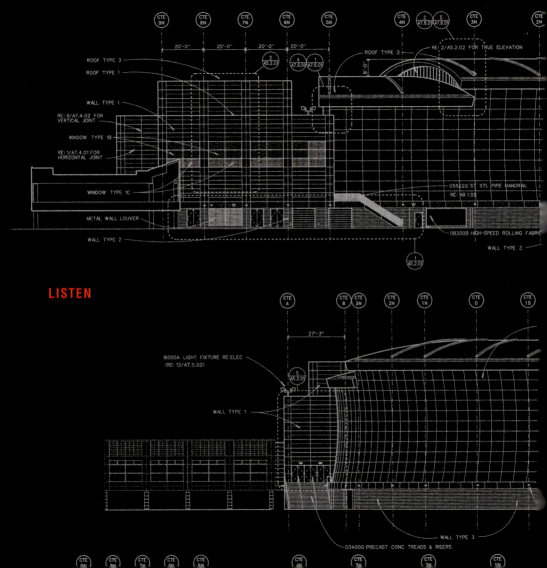

LISTEN

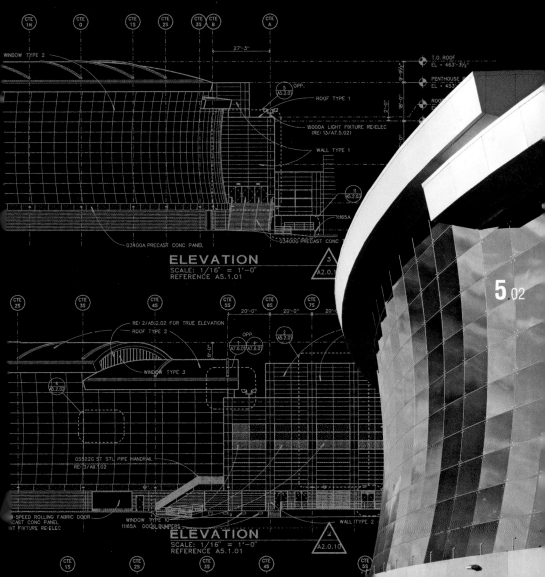

The public process can actually give life to a project. There are so many stakeholders with so many opinions that you get the opportunity to do what's best.

LISTEN

The bigger the project, the greater the demand for credibility that you are required to meet.

This translates into TRUST on the job and greater creativity.

LISTEN

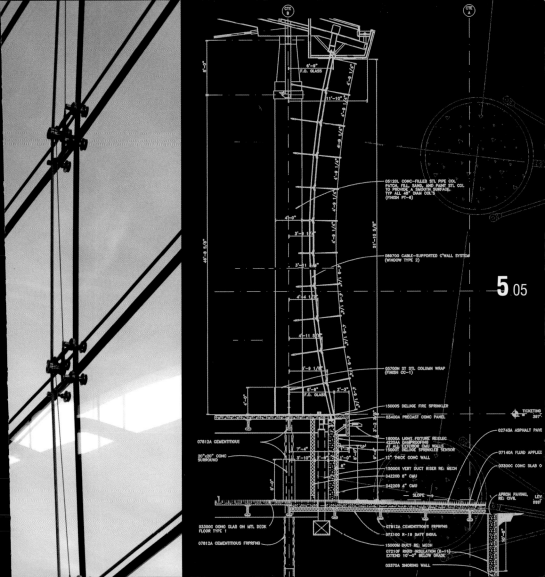

LISTEN

In architecture, creativity is about **RECEIVING WITH INTENT**. You go through a rigorous, rational and disciplined search. Your reward, if you are open to it, is an unexpected, yet perfect, solution.

5.07

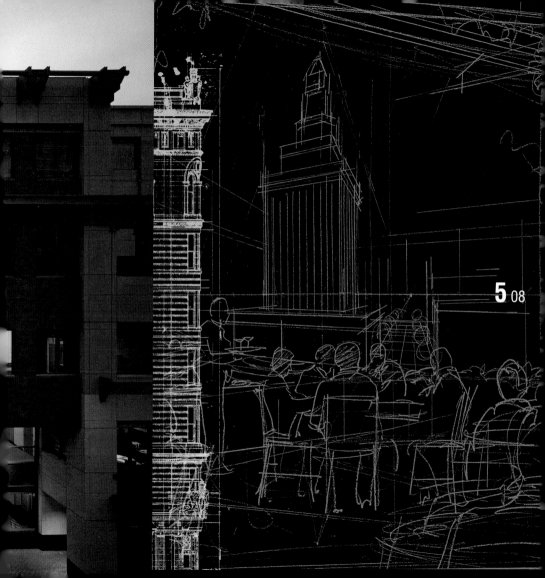
5 08

LISTEN

DETAILS OF EXTERIOR.
FIRST NATIONAL BANK BUILDING
OAKLAND CAL.

SCALE 3/8"=1'-0"   L.D. DUTTON · ARCHITECT

LISTEN

LISTEN

LISTEN

UNITY

VOICES

RECEIVE

OPENNESS

COMMITMENT

5 13

LISTEN

5.14

5.15

LISTEN CLOSELY

DISCOVER THE NATURAL ORDER

USE CONTEXT TO CREATE AN IDENTITY

LET CULTURE GUIDE DESIGN

CELEBRATE THE ENTRY

STAY FOCUSED

RESTRAIN THE EGO

DESIGN FOR PEOPLE

06
STAY FOCUSED

- Vision
- Balance
- Patience
- Discipline
- Determination

The public process can be long, protracted, bureaucratic, complex and vulnerable to political upheaval. It brings together diverse groups of people with many agendas.

After years of experience in the public arena, I understand that an exceptional building requires a thorough process. It also requires discipline and patience, which are key to my "Patient Search."

This means concentrating on the end goal and avoiding the distraction of day-to-day "noise." It also requires active participation, the need to listen, to stay balanced. We pay strict attention to detail and clear lines of communication.

It's all about the big picture. Give the community a building that serves well for years to come.

FOCUS

Our "Patient Search" approach is not a long, iterative process. Often it is very compact.

We keep coming up with ideas upon ideas. The best ones become evident and quickly mature. The process feels like a scientific exploration at first, and...

the result is ALCHEMY.

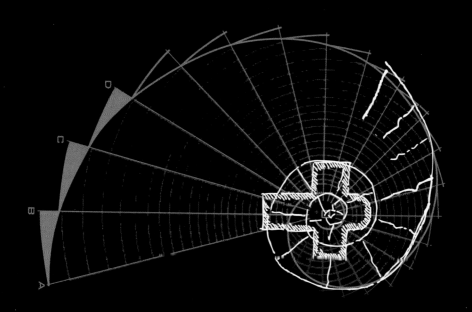

FOCUS

FOCUS

6 05

FOCUS

6 06

FOCUS

VISION

BALANCE

PATIENCE

DISCIPLINE

DETERMINATION

FOCUS

A bold architectural statement turns a public building into a landmark, but it is in the details where the architect becomes THE REAL STORYTELLER.

6.08

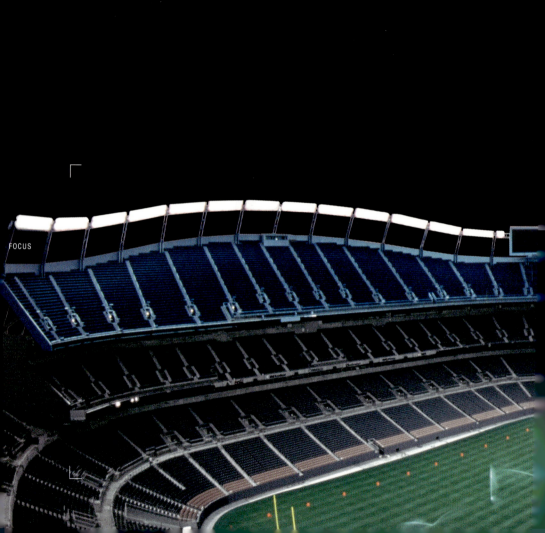

FOCUS   **WHEN DESIGNING, STAY FLUID. STAY OPEN.**

6.10

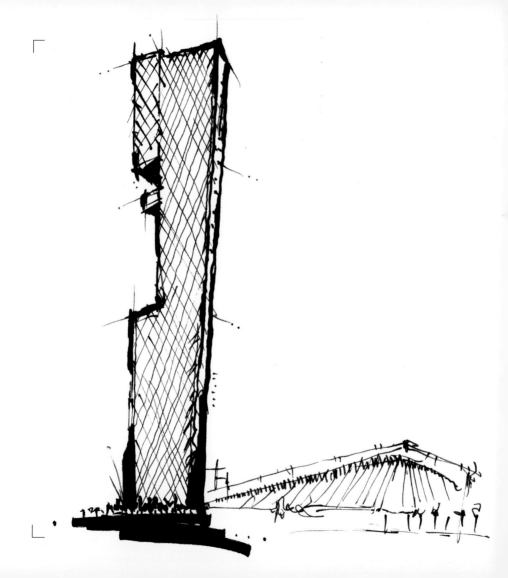

VISION

BALANCE

PATIENCE **6**.11

DISCIPLINE

DETERMINATION

FOCUS

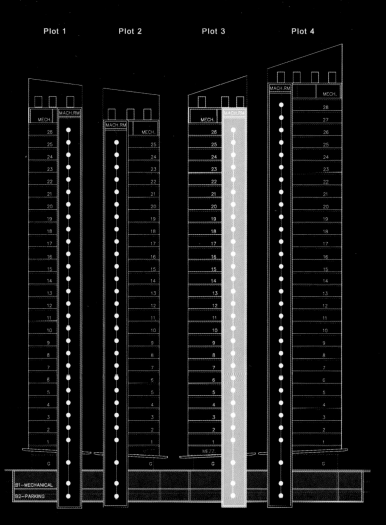

FOCUS

SIMPLICITY ALWAYS TRUMPS CONFUSION.

6.13

FOCUS

FOCUS

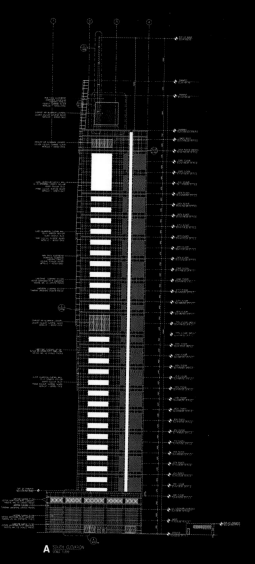

STAY FOCUSED

DISCOVER THE NATURAL ORDER

USE CONTEXT TO CREATE AN IDENTITY

LET CULTURE GUIDE DESIGN

CELEBRATE THE ENTRY

LISTEN CLOSELY

RESTRAIN THE EGO

DESIGN FOR PEOPLE

6.16

0 7

> Discipline
> Sensitivity
> Humanistic
> Self-control
> Pragmatism

RESTRAIN THE EGO

A public building is part of the story of a community. It needs to tell its own tale, but never overpower its purpose or the people who use it.

A building is not the autobiography of an architect.

My role is that of pragmatist, employing common sense and uncommon sensitivity to bring together every element that becomes the design.

People are why a public building exists. That's why the humanistic aspects of our approach are an essential element in our design of civic buildings. Community, site and program unite to speak through us. Those forces then combine to create a compelling building, where the fruit of discipline is the balance of design and function.

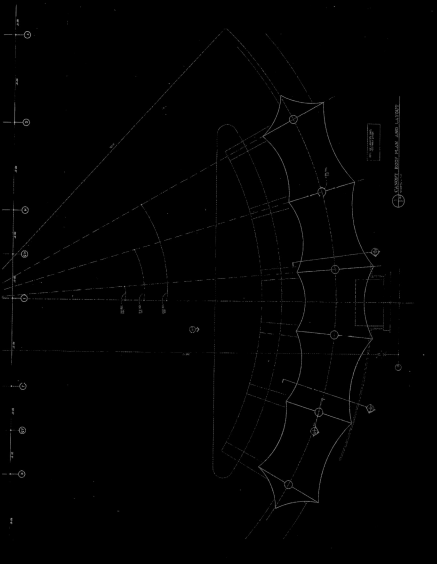

RESTRAINT

The real art of iconic public architecture is getting people to see **THEIR OWN GREATNESS** in a building.

7 03

RESTRAINT

RESTRAINT

DISCIPLINE

SENSITIVITY

HUMANISTIC

SELF-CONTROL

PRAGMATISM

7.05

Pragmatism is THE HEART of every great building, but no one should ever feel it beating.

7.06

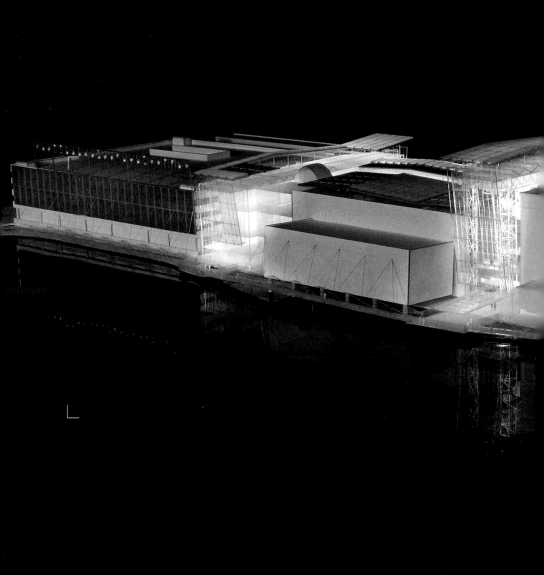

7 07

RESTRAINT

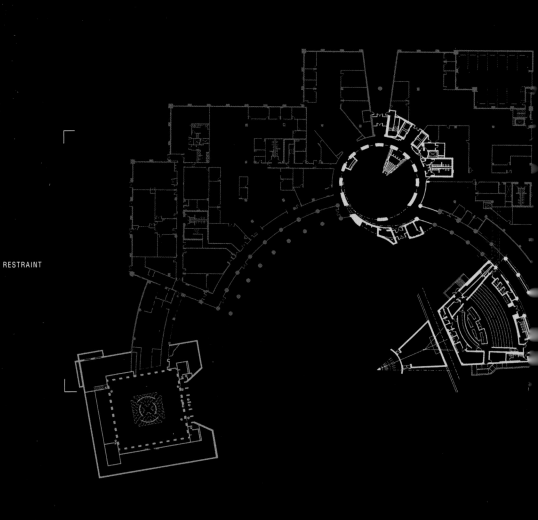

7.09

7.10

RESTRAINT

7.13

RESTRAINT

DISCIPLINE

SENSITIVITY

HUMANISTIC

SELF-CONTROL

PRAGMATISM

7.14

RESTRAIN THE EGO

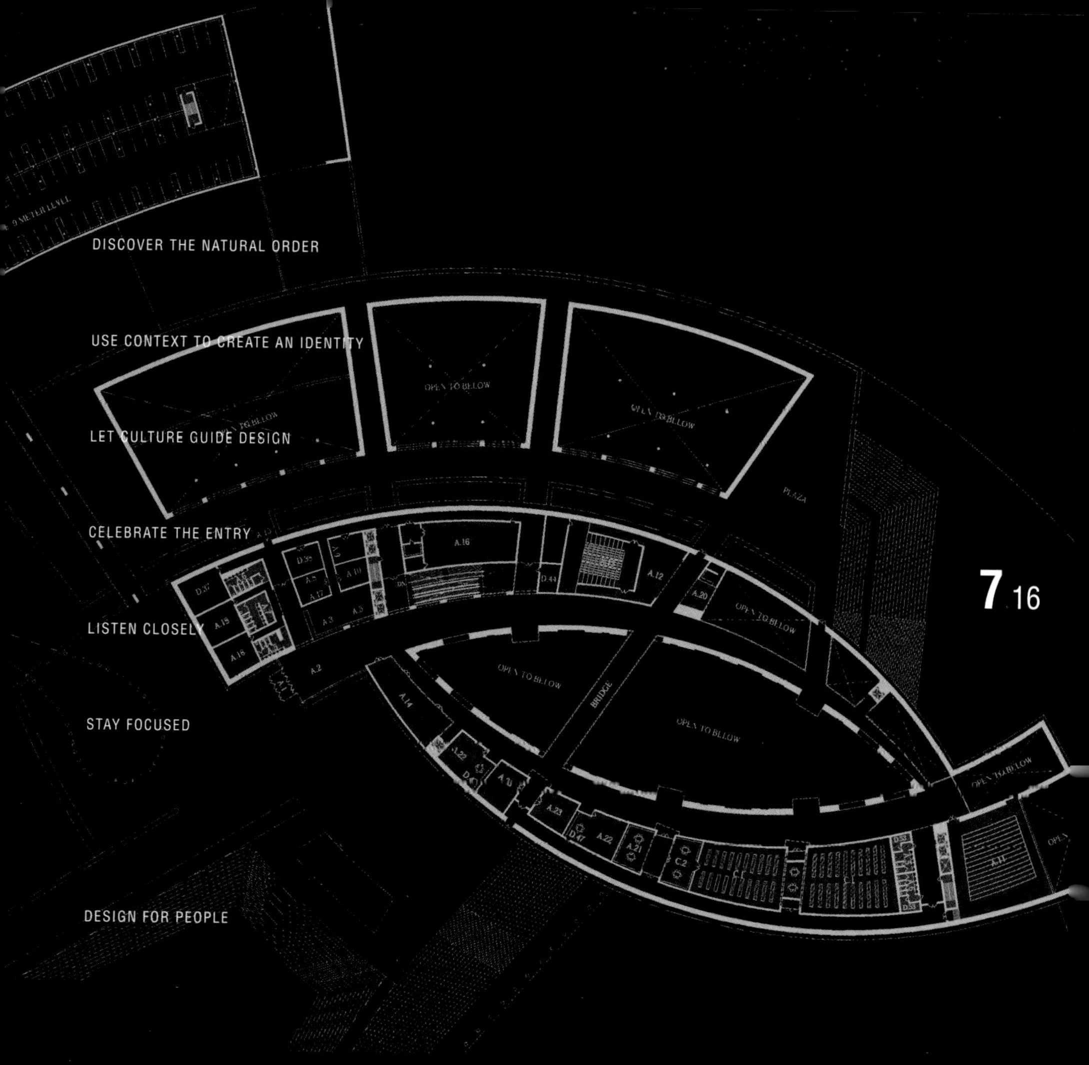

DISCOVER THE NATURAL ORDER

USE CONTEXT TO CREATE AN IDENTITY

LET CULTURE GUIDE DESIGN

CELEBRATE THE ENTRY

LISTEN CLOSELY

STAY FOCUSED

DESIGN FOR PEOPLE

7.16

- Timelessness
- Universal Truth
- Confluence
- Conscientious
- Design to Last

DESIGN FOR PEOPLE

My first seven Touchstones of Design speak to the process of bringing aesthetic excellence and distinction to public buildings.

The final Touchstone sets the stage for what lies ahead — the infinite aspects of great public architecture.

The future is built on intangible factors such as dreams and inspiration, but it is made real through architecture.

Truly great architecture is not controlled by catchphrases of the times. It transcends time and space. It shows genuine respect for the environment, for people and for the universe. It is, in short, about design that elevates and restores. It is about design that lasts.

This is the confluence of my Touchstones of Design, the place where function meets art in a building that is both timeless and memorable.

Public architecture is designed by people for people, now, and for generations to come.

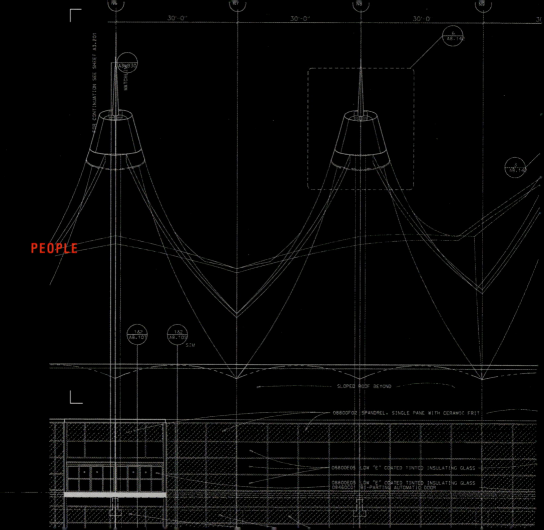

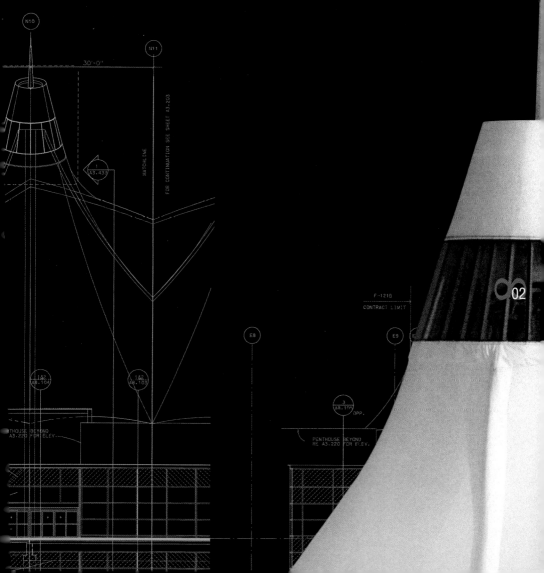

PEOPLE

An architect must think in many dimensions. In addition to the physical, every thought has a dimension of time and timelessness. Then construction and manufacturing enter in – how do the phases flow together? Money – where do you conserve, where do you make a statement? There are many stresses – structural, seismic, wind load...

...All the while you must stay aware of **THE HUMAN EXPERIENCE** you are creating.

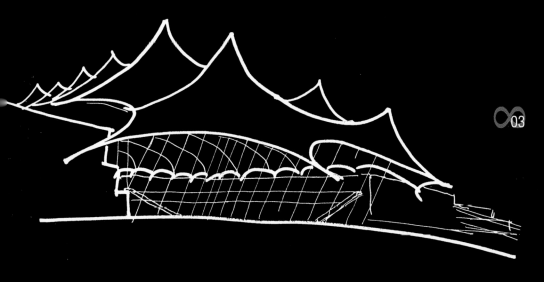

PEOPLE

∞.04

PEOPLE

TIMELESSNESS

UNIVERSAL TRUTH

CONFLUENCE

CONSCIENTIOUS

DESIGN TO LAST

PEOPLE

06

PEOPLE

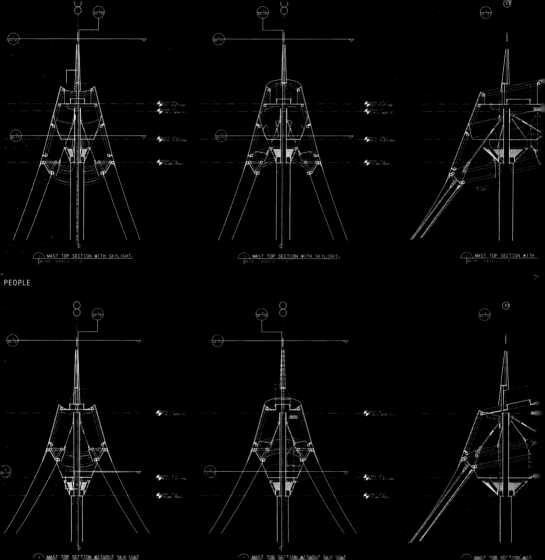

PEOPLE

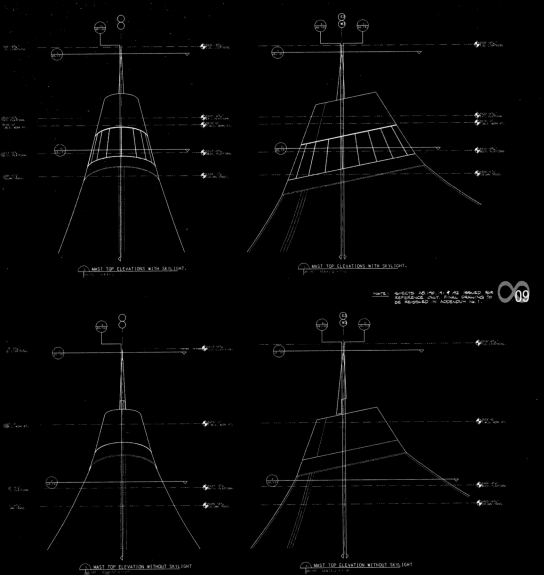

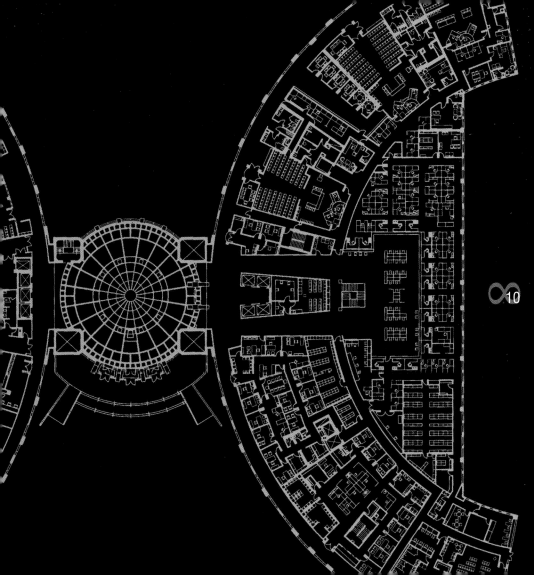

PEOPLE

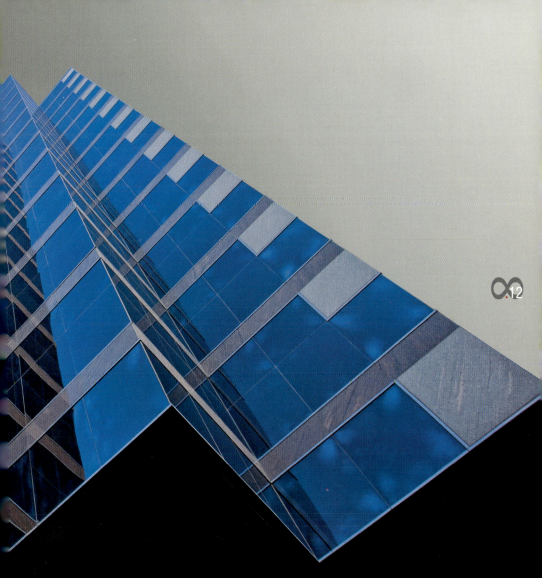

PEOPLE

PEOPLE

14

BIOGRAPHY

Curtis Fentress was born to a family living on a tobacco farm – between two small communities – Summerfield and Oakridge – in North Carolina. In high school he gravitated to drafting and engineering. Hard work enabled him to attend the College of Design at North Carolina State University, where he graduated with honors with a Bachelor of Architecture degree.

After leaving a position with I.M. Pei, Fentress joined the newly formed firm Kohn Pedersen Fox to continue his pursuit of large-scale public projects while striving to bring humanism to civic buildings.

"Public buildings involve process and commitment, periods of reflection and flashes of illumination," he says. Curtis Fentress' commitment to designing for people has been honored by the American Institute of Architects with the 2010 Thomas Jefferson Award for Public Architecture. This prestigious award recognizes one architect in the private sector with a portfolio of accomplishments that evidences great depth while making a significant contribution to the quality of public architecture.

KPF sent Fentress to Colorado in the late 1970s as project designer for a 36-story tower in Denver. In *1980 Building Design and Construction* magazine named him "Young Professional of the Year." Attracted by the natural beauty of Colorado, Fentress founded his own firm that year and later was awarded the opportunity to design Denver International Airport. His iconic Teflon™-coated, peaked-roof design – voted "Best Airport in North America" and fourth "Favorite American Architecture" – propelled him into the international realm.

Fentress designed Incheon International Airport in South Korea, voted the "World's Best Airport" by Skytrax's World Airport Awards in 2009, based on a survey of almost 9 million airline passengers. Incheon also has been voted "World's Best Airport" four consecutive years by 200,000 world travelers polled by Airports Council International. In the United States, Fentress has earned acclaim for the distinctive design of the National Museum of the Marine Corps in Greater Washington, D.C., which has won 20 awards for innovation and design excellence in its first 23 months. In 30 years of practice, the firm has received more than 300 awards. Fentress Architects' work has been recognized in countless news and trade publications and numerous books worldwide. The latter include 11 books dedicated to the studio's work – including several that Images Publishing has been proud to be associated with.

The impact of civic buildings on people has led Fentress to make public architecture his area of expertise. Through years of experience, he has developed his "Patient Search" approach, a meticulous process of discovery that he and his design team follow through immersion in influences such as context and community. This approach envisions the balance of art and function in timeless public architecture, using the power of cultural references to attract and unify people.

The design studio is guided by the 8 Touchstones of Design, a set of principles that addresses both the practical side of creating public architecture as well as the more aspirational implications of timeless design and conscientious practices.

"Some architects have a preconceived notion of what a building should be – they design from the outside like the building is a piece of sculpture. I prefer to patiently search through extensive discovery until I find a seam somewhere, crack it open and discover the art inside," says Fentress, FAIA, RIBA, principal in charge of design.

TEAM

ABBEYWILLIAMS ADRIANA ZARRILLO AGATHA KESSLER AGNES WONG AL RUBER
SALEX KNOWLES ALEX THOME ALEXA TAYLOR ALIKA BROOKS ALVIN PASTRANA AM
BER STEWART AMY SOLOMON ANDRE VITE ANN ROY BENCE KOVACS BEVERLY PAX BILL
DILATUSH BOB OUDEN BRAD WONNACOTT BRANDON LUCERO BRIAN GHAFFEL BR
ANNA BOWLIN BRYAN KRISTOF BRYAN SMITH CARL GOODIEL CAROL CARR CAROL KC
PLIN CHARLES CANNON CHRIS LYNCH CHRIS PETERS CHRIS ROONEY CHRISTINE RA
PAL CHRISTOPHER CAMPBELL CLOVER COREY OCHSNER COURTNEY HOLLOHAN
CURT ENTRESS DAVE TIDEY DAVID HOFMANN DAVID MECHAM DAVID WOO DEBBIE
OBERTS DEBORAH LUCKING DEE RENDON DEREK PRICE DYLAN MCQUINN ELIZABETH
TURNER EMILY FINCH EMMETT HARRISON ERIC LIND ERIC ZENONI EVAN MILLER FER
NANDO SANTOS GREG BILLINGHAM HOLLY CARSON JACK COOK JACLYN WENAAS JAR
ED BLANK JASON KNOWLES JASON LOUI JAYNE COBURN JEFF OLSON JEFFREY ANGLA
DA JENNIFER GEE JENNIFER ITO JEREMY PHILLIPS JESSE DZIERZANOWSKI JESSICA
SEITZ JI-HYUN KIM JIM SOBEY JOHN STOLTZE JORDAN ROOS JOSEPH TONSAGER KARA
ELLIOTT KAREN GILBERT KAREN MILLER KARL LEONARD KELLY DUNN KELLY MASTRO
MAURO KEVIN DURHAM KEVIN HANDLEY KEVIN MUMFORD KIRSTEN SCHARNELL KRIS
TEN HURTY KRISTEN SHOUP KRISTINE ROUSE LAURA GRAFE LAUREN LEIF THOM
AS LES STUART LINDA HOPKINS LYNDSAY SABAKA MALYSA MARTINEZ MARC DIETRICH
MARIANNE REYNOLDS MARIO FIGUEROA MARISA PICARD MARK MCPHERSON MARK
MCQUISTION MARK OUTMAN MARK RUTHMAN MARK WAGNER MARTIN EISS MAR
CHANDLER MATTHEW BREEST MATTHEW ONEGGER MATTHEW JOHNSON MATTHEW
POPOWSKI MELANIE FLORES MELANIE KUHN MEREDITH LONG MICHAEL GENGLER M
CHAEL OLINGER MICHELLE LOFANO MIKALA LASMIKE WALTER NATE KIBLER S
NICOLE COCHRAN COLE ROAN TREE OLIVER WISCHMEYER PA
PAUL LACLAIR WENGER REED GOODRICK TALLEY ROBIN
ROLAND RYAN CHEN SCOTT TLE SHARLENE HYUN SONNY WI
SPENCER BEAR STEVE CO ADSTEVE CU MMINGS STEVE KUNIN SUE ZAYNARD
SYLVIA MCLEAN TAMARA STRICKLAND THOM WALSH TIM GARRICK
TODD BRITTON TOM THEOBALD TRACY MATTESON TYLER WALLACE TYMMIE BYRAM
ROBERTS WENDY GOSSETT YE KATERINA TERI ETSKAYA ZACHARY

30

YEARS OF FENTRESS ARCHITECTS
INSPIRED DESIGN FOR PEOPLE

300

MILLION ANNUAL
VISITORS

143
MILLION SQ FT

22.7
BILLION DOLLARS
OF DESIGN

149 CIVIC PROJECTS

79 OFFICE BUILDINGS

61 MIXED-USE PROJECTS

60 RENOVATION AND PRESERVATION

42 DESIGN-BUILD PROJECTS

41 HIGH-RISE BUILDINGS

91.6 MILLION SQ FT

31.4 MILLION SQ FT

34 MILLION SQ FT

6.4 MILLION SQ FT

11.8 MILLION SQ FT

18.4 MILLION SQ FT

38	MUSEUMS
19	INTERNATIONAL AIRPORTS
16	LABORATORIES
14	CONVENTION CENTERS
12	COURTHOUSES
11	HIGHER EDUCATION

3.9 MILLION SQ FT

51.4 MILLION SQ FT

4.3 MILLION SQ FT

8.7 MILLION SQ FT

3.7 MILLION SQ FT

1.7 MILLION SQ FT

300
DESIGN & INNOVATION
HONORS & AWARDS

33

INTERNATIONAL DESIGN
COMPETITIONS
WON

40

YEARS OF DESIGN
JUST THE BEGINNING

CREDITS

**Denver International Airport
Passenger Terminal Complex**
Denver, CO, USA

Fentress Architects
+ Pouw & Associates
+ Bertram A. Bruton & Associates

Photo: Timothy Hursley

**San Jose International Airport
Terminal B** [+A+C+CONRAC]
San Jose, CA, USA

Fentress Architects

© 2009 Fentress Architects

**National Museum
of the Marine Corps**
Quantico, VA, USA

Fentress Architects

Photo: Nick Merrick
© Hedrich Blessing

Curtis Fentress
at **Home**

Fentress Architects

Photo: Chris Humphreys
Photography, Inc.

1.02
natural order

Incheon International Airport
Passenger Terminal Complex
Seoul, South Korea

Fentress Architects
+ Korean Architects Collaborative International

Photo: Nick Merrick
© Hedrich Blessing

.04
natural order

Incheon International Airport
Passenger Terminal Complex
Seoul, South Korea

Fentress Architects
+ Korean Architects Collaborative International

Photo: Nick Merrick
© Hedrich Blessing

.05
natural order

Incheon International Airport
Passenger Terminal Complex
Seoul, South Korea

Fentress Architects
+ Korean Architects Collaborative International

Photo: Lisa Hillmer
© Fentress Architects

.06
natural order

Incheon International Airport
Passenger Terminal Complex
Seoul, South Korea

Fentress Architects
+ Korean Architects Collaborative International

Photo: Jeff Goldberg / Esto

.07
natural order

Incheon International Airport
Passenger Terminal Complex
Seoul, South Korea

Fentress Architects
+ Korean Architects Collaborative International

Photo: Nick Merrick
© Hedrich Blessing

.08
natural order

Incheon International Airport
Passenger Terminal Complex
Seoul, South Korea

Fentress Architects
+ Korean Architects Collaborative International

Photo: Jeff Goldberg / Esto

.09
natural order

Incheon International Airport
Passenger Terminal Complex
Seoul, South Korea

Fentress Architects
+ Korean Architects Collaborative International

Photo: Lisa Hillmer
© Fentress Architects

1.10
natural order

Jefferson County Government Center
Golden, CO, USA

Fentress Architects

Photo: Nick Merrick
© Hedrich Blessing

.11
natural order

Jefferson County Government Center
Golden, CO, USA

Fentress Architects

Photo: Nick Merrick
© Hedrich Blessing

.12
natural order

Raleigh-Durham International Airport
Raleigh-Durham, NC, USA

Fentress Architects

Photo: Nick Merrick
© Hedrich Blessing

.13
natural order

Raleigh-Durham International Airport
Raleigh-Durham, NC, USA

Fentress Architects

Photo: Nick Merrick
© Hedrich Blessing

Raleigh-Durham International Airport
Raleigh-Durham, NC, USA

Fentress Architects

Photo: Nick Merrick
© Hedrich Blessing

.14
natural order

San Joaquin County Administration Building
Stockton, CA, USA

Fentress Architects

Photo: Jason A. Knowles
© Fentress Architects

San Joaquin County Administration Building
Stockton, CA, USA

Fentress Architects

Photo: Jason A. Knowles
© Fentress Architects

.15
natural order

San Joaquin County Administration Building
Stockton, CA, USA

Fentress Architects

Photo: Jason A. Knowles
© Fentress Architects

.16
natural order

San Joaquin County Administration Building
Stockton, CA, USA

Fentress Architects

Photo: Jason A. Knowles
© Fentress Architects

.02 context

National Museum
of Wildlife Art
Jackson, WY, USA

Fentress Architects

Photo: Jeff Goldberg / Esto

.04 context

National Museum
of Wildlife Art
Jackson, WY, USA

Fentress Architects

Photo: Jeff Goldberg / Esto

.05 context

National Museum
of Wildlife Art
Jackson, WY, USA

Fentress Architects

Photo: Nick Merrick
© Hedrich Blessing

.06 context

National Museum
of Wildlife Art
Jackson, WY, USA

Fentress Architects

Photo: Nick Merrick
© Hedrich Blessing

.07 context

National Museum
of Wildlife Art
Jackson, WY, USA

Fentress Architects

© 2009 Fentress Architects

.08 context

Palm Springs
Convention Center
Palm Springs, CA, USA

Fentress Architects

Photo: Nick Merrick
© Hedrich Blessing

.09 context

Palm Springs
Convention Center
Palm Springs, CA, USA

Fentress Architects

Photo courtesy of
Palm Springs Convention Center

2.10 context

Palm Springs
Convention Center
Palm Springs, CA, USA

Fentress Architects

Photo: Nick Merrick
© Hedrich Blessing

Palm Springs
Convention Center
Palm Springs, CA, USA

Fentress Architects

Photo: Nick Merrick
© Hedrich Blessing

.11 context

Palm Springs
Convention Center
Palm Springs, CA, USA

Fentress Architects

Photo: Nick Merrick
© Hedrich Blessing

.12 context

Los Angeles Int'l Airport
Master Plan + Int'l Terminal
+ Modernization
Los Angeles, CA, USA

Fentress Architects
+ HNTB Architecture, Inc.

© 2009 Fentress Architects

.13 context

Los Angeles Int'l Airport
Master Plan + Int'l Terminal
+ Modernization
Los Angeles, CA, USA

Fentress Architects
+ HNTB Architecture, Inc.

© 2009 Fentress Architects

.14 context

Los Angeles Int'l Airport
Master Plan + Int'l Terminal
+ Modernization
Los Angeles, CA, USA

Fentress Architects
+ HNTB Architecture, Inc.

Photo: Jason A. Knowles
© Fentress Architects

.15 context

Los Angeles Int'l Airport
Master Plan + Int'l Terminal
+ Modernization
Los Angeles, CA, USA

Fentress Architects
+ HNTB Architecture, Inc.

Photo: Jason A. Knowles
© Fentress Architects

.16 context

Sanford Consortium
for Regenerative Medicine
La Jolla, CA, USA

Fentress Architects
+ Davis Davis Architects

© 2009 Fentress Architects

3.02 culture

National Museum of the Marine Corps
Quantico, VA, USA

Fentress Architects

Photo: Nick Merrick
© Hedrich Blessing

.04 culture

National Museum of the Marine Corps
Quantico, VA, USA

Fentress Architects

Photo: James P. Scholz

.05 culture

National Museum of the Marine Corps
Quantico, VA, USA

Fentress Architects

Photo: Jason A. Knowles
© Fentress Architects

National Museum of the Marine Corps
Quantico, VA, USA

Photo: Joe Rosenthal,
AP/Wide World Photos

.06 culture

National Museum of the Marine Corps
Quantico, VA, USA

Fentress Architects

Photo: Nick Merrick
© Hedrich Blessing

National Museum of the Marine Corps
Quantico, VA, USA

Fentress Architects

Photo: James P. Scholz

.07 culture

National Museum of the Marine Corps
Quantico, VA, USA

Fentress Architects

Photo: James P. Scholz

.08 culture

Peery's Egyptian Theater Renovation
Ogden, UT, USA

Fentress Architects
+ Sanders Herman Architects

Photo: Steve Hall
© Hedrich Blessing

.09 culture

Peery's Egyptian Theater Renovation
Ogden, UT, USA

Fentress Architects
+ Sanders Herman Architects

Photo: Steve Hall
© Hedrich Blessing

Peery's Egyptian Theater Renovation
Ogden, UT, USA

Fentress Architects
+ Sanders Herman Architects

Photo: Steve Hall
© Hedrich Blessing

3.10 culture

U.S. Federal Courthouse
Cape Girardeau, MO, USA

Fentress Architects

Photo: James P. Scholz

.11 culture

The Chapel at Cherry Hills Community Church
Highlands Ranch, CO, USA

Fentress Architects

Photo: © Ben Tremper Photography

.12 culture

The Chapel at Cherry Hills Community Church
Highlands Ranch, CO, USA

Fentress Architects

Photo: © Ben Tremper Photography

.13 culture

Santa Fe Community Convention Center
Santa Fe, NM, USA

Fentress Architects
+ Spears Architects

Photo: Nick Merrick
© Hedrich Blessing

.14 culture

Santa Fe Community Convention Center
Santa Fe, NM, USA

Fentress Architects
+ Spears Architects

Photo: Nick Merrick
© Hedrich Blessing

.15 culture

Santa Fe Community Convention Center
Santa Fe, NM, USA

Fentress Architects
+ Spears Architects

Photo: Nick Merrick
© Hedrich Blessing

Santa Fe Community Convention Center
Santa Fe, NM, USA

Fentress Architects
+ Spears Architects

Photo: © Ben Tremper Photography

.16 culture

Santa Fe Community Convention Center
Santa Fe, NM, USA

Fentress Architects
+ Spears Architects

Photo: Nick Merrick
© Hedrich Blessing

4.02 entry

**Colorado
Convention Center**
Denver, CO, USA

Fentress Architects
+ Bertram A. Bruton & Associates
+ Harold Massop Associates
+ Abo Copeland Architecture

Photo: Ron Johnson

.04 entry

**Colorado
Convention Center**
Denver, CO, USA

Fentress Architects
+ Bertram A. Bruton & Associates
+ Harold Massop Associates
+ Abo Copeland Architecture

Photo: © Scott Dressel-Martin

.05 entry

**Colorado
Convention Center**
Denver, CO, USA

Fentress Architects
+ Bertram A. Bruton & Associates
+ Harold Massop Associates
+ Abo Copeland Architecture

Photo: Ron Johnson

.06 entry

**Colorado
Convention Center**
Denver, CO, USA

Fentress Architects
+ Bertram A. Bruton & Associates
+ Harold Massop Associates
+ Abo Copeland Architecture

Photo: Nick Merrick
© Hedrich Blessing

.07 entry

**Colorado
Convention Center**
Denver, CO, USA

Fentress Architects
+ Bertram A. Bruton & Associates
+ Harold Massop Associates
+ Abo Copeland Architecture

Photo: Ron Johnson

.08 entry

**Colorado
Convention Center**
Denver, CO, USA

Fentress Architects
+ Bertram A. Bruton & Associates
+ Harold Massop Associates
+ Abo Copeland Architecture

Photo: Ron Johnson

**Colorado
Convention Center**
Denver, CO, USA

Fentress Architects
+ Bertram A. Bruton & Associates
+ Harold Massop Associates
+ Abo Copeland Architecture

Photo: Jason A. Knowles
© Fentress Architects
Sculpture: Bernar Venet

.09 entry

**Colorado
Convention Center**
Denver, CO, USA

Fentress Architects
+ Bertram A. Bruton & Associates
+ Harold Massop Associates
+ Abo Copeland Architecture

Photo: James P. Scholz
Sculpture: Lawrence Argent

.10 entry

Pasadena
Convention Center
Pasadena, CA, USA

Fentress Architects
+ Miralles Associates, Inc.

© 2009 Fentress Architects

.11 entry

Pasadena
Convention Center
Pasadena, CA, USA

Fentress Architects
+ Miralles Associates, Inc.

Photo: © Chip Raches

.12 entry

Pasadena
Convention Center
Pasadena, CA, USA

Fentress Architects
+ Miralles Associates, Inc.

Photo: © Chip Raches

.13 entry

Pasadena
Convention Center
Pasadena, CA, USA

Fentress Architects
+ Miralles Associates, Inc.

Photo: © Ben Tremper Photography

.14 entry

Pasadena
Convention Center
Pasadena, CA, USA

Fentress Architects
+ Miralles Associates, Inc.

Photo: © Ben Tremper Photography

.15 entry

Pasadena
Convention Center
Pasadena, CA, USA

Fentress Architects
+ Miralles Associates, Inc.

Photo: © Chip Raches

.16 entry

Regional Transportation
Commission & Flood Control
District Headquarters
Las Vegas, NV, USA

Fentress Architects
+ Robert A. Felden, Inc

Photo: Nick Merrick

5.02 listen

Seattle-Tacoma International
Airport Central Terminal
Expansion + Redevelopment
Seattle, WA, USA

Fentress Architects
+ Streeter & Associates Architects

Photo: Nick Merrick
© Hedrich Blessing

.03 listen

Seattle-Tacoma International
Airport Central Terminal
Expansion + Redevelopment
Seattle, WA, USA

Fentress Architects
+ Streeter & Associates Architects

Photo: Nick Merrick
© Hedrich Blessing

.04 listen

Seattle-Tacoma International
Airport Central Terminal
Expansion + Redevelopment
Seattle, WA, USA

Fentress Architects
+ Streeter & Associates Architects

Photo: James P. Scholz

.05 listen

Seattle-Tacoma International
Airport Central Terminal
Expansion + Redevelopment
Seattle, WA, USA

Fentress Architects
+ Streeter & Associates Architects

Photo: Nick Merrick
© Hedrich Blessing

.06 listen

Seattle-Tacoma International
Airport Central Terminal
Expansion + Redevelopment
Seattle, WA, USA

Fentress Architects
+ Streeter & Associates Architects

Photo: Nick Merrick
© Hedrich Blessing

.07 listen

Oakland Admin. Buildings
Oakland, CA, USA

Fentress Architects
+ Y.H. Lee Associates, Architects
+ Muller & Caulfield
+ Gerson/Overstreet

Photo: © Mikki Piper

.08 listen

Oakland Admin. Buildings
Oakland, CA, USA

Fentress Architects
+ Y.H. Lee Associates, Architects
+ Muller & Caulfield
+ Gerson/Overstreet

Photo: Nick Merrick
© Hedrich Blessing

5.09 listen

Oakland Admin. Buildings
Oakland, CA, USA

Fentress Architects
+ Y.H. Lee Associates, Architects
+ Muller & Caulfield
+ Gerson/Overstreet

Photo: Nick Merrick
© Hedrich Blessing

Oakland Admin. Buildings
Oakland, CA, USA

Fentress Architects
+ Y.H. Lee Associates, Architects
+ Muller & Caulfield
+ Gerson/Overstreet

Photo: Nick Merrick
© Hedrich Blessing

.10 listen

Oakland Admin. Buildings
Oakland, CA, USA

Fentress Architects
+ Y.H. Lee Associates, Architects
+ Muller & Caulfield
+ Gerson/Overstreet

Photo: Nick Merrick
© Hedrich Blessing

.11 listen

Oakland Admin. Buildings
Oakland, CA, USA

Fentress Architects
+ Y.H. Lee Associates, Architects
+ Muller & Caulfield
+ Gerson/Overstreet

Photo: Nick Merrick
© Hedrich Blessing

Oakland Admin. Buildings
Oakland, CA, USA

Fentress Architects
+ Y.H. Lee Associates, Architects
+ Muller & Caulfield
+ Gerson/Overstreet

Photo: Nick Merrick
© Hedrich Blessing

.12 listen

Oakland Admin. Buildings
Oakland, CA, USA

Fentress Architects
+ Y.H. Lee Associates, Architects
+ Muller & Caulfield
+ Gerson/Overstreet

Photo: Nick Merrick
© Hedrich Blessing

.14 listen

Natural Resources Building
+ Laboratories
Olympia, WA, USA

Fentress Architects

Photo: Thorney Lieberman

Natural Resources Building
+ Laboratories
Olympia, WA, USA

Fentress Architects

Photo: Thorney Lieberman

.15 listen

David E. Skaggs Research
Center >> NOAA
Boulder, CO, USA

Fentress Architects

Photo: Nick Merrick
© Hedrich Blessing

David E. Skaggs Research
Center >> NOAA
Boulder, CO, USA

Fentress Architects

Photo: Ron Johnson

.16 listen

University of California
Irvine Humanities Gateway
Irvine, CA, USA

Fentress Architects

© 2009 Fentress Architects

6.02 focus
1999 Broadway Office Building
Denver, CO, USA

Fentress Architects

Photo: Nick Merrick
© Hedrich Blessing

.04 focus
1999 Broadway Office Building
Denver, CO, USA

Fentress Architects

Photo: © Ken Paul

.05 focus
1999 Broadway Office Building
Denver, CO, USA

Fentress Architects

Photo: © Ken Paul

.06 focus
1999 Broadway Office Building
Denver, CO, USA

Fentress Architects

Photo: Nick Merrick
© Hedrich Blessing

1999 Broadway Office Building
Denver, CO, USA

Fentress Architects

Photo: Nick Merrick
© Hedrich Blessing

.07 focus
INVESCO Field at Mile High
Denver, CO, USA

Fentress Architects
+ HNTB Sports Entertainment
+ Bertram A. Bruton & Associates

Photo: © Tony Eitzel
Denver Panoramic

.08 focus
INVESCO Field at Mile High
Denver, CO, USA

Fentress Architects
+ HNTB Sports Entertainment
+ Bertram A. Bruton & Associates

Photo: © Jackie Shumaker

.09 focus
INVESCO Field at Mile High
Denver, CO, USA

Fentress Architects
+ HNTB Sports Entertainment
+ Bertram A. Bruton & Associates

Photo: © Jackie Shumaker

6 focus

10

Bell Tower
Denver, CO, USA

Fentress Architects

© 2009 Fentress Architects

11
KIA Headquarters Building
Kuwait City, Kuwait

Fentress Architects

© 2009 Fentress Architects

12
Kuwait Business Town High Rise Office Towers
Al Sharq, Kuwait

Fentress Architects

© 2009 Fentress Architects

13

Bonn Postal Headquarters Design Competition
Bonn, Germany

Fentress Architects

Photo: Ron Johnson

14

Arraya Center Office Tower
Kuwait City, Kuwait

Fentress Architects

© 2009 Fentress Architects

Arraya Center Office Tower
Kuwait City, Kuwait

Fentress Architects

Photo: Pawel Sulima / PACE

15

Baitek Mixed-Use Tower
Kuwait City, Kuwait

Fentress Architects

Photo: Curtis Fentress
© Fentress Architects

16
Dubai Mixed-Use Development
Dubai, United Arab Emirates

Fentress Architects

© 2009 Fentress Architects

Dubai Mixed-Use Development
Dubai, United Arab Emirates

Fentress Architects

© 2009 Fentress Architects

7.
restrain

.02 restrain

National Cowboy and Western Heritage Museum
Oklahoma City, OK, USA

Fentress Architects

Photo: Timothy Hursley

.04 restrain

National Cowboy and Western Heritage Museum
Oklahoma City, OK, USA

Fentress Architects

Photo: Timothy Hursley

National Cowboy and Western Heritage Museum
Oklahoma City, OK, USA

Fentress Architects

Photo: © Ben Tremper Photography

.05 restrain

National Cowboy and Western Heritage Museum
Oklahoma City, OK, USA

Fentress Architects

Photo: Timothy Hursley

.06 restrain

Museum of Science
Boston, MA, USA

Fentress Architects
+ LDA Architects
+ Cambridge Seven Associates, Inc

© 2009 Fentress Architects

.07 restrain

Museum of Science
Boston, MA, USA

Fentress Architects
+ LDA Architects
+ Cambridge Seven Associates, Inc.

Photo: Jason A. Knowles
© Fentress Architects

.08 restrain

Museum of Science
Boston, MA, USA

Fentress Architects
+ LDA Architects
+ Cambridge Seven Associates, Inc.

Photo: © Greg Premru 2007

.09 restrain

Clark County Government Center
Las Vegas, NV, USA

Fentress Architects
+ Domingo Cambeiro Corporation

Photo: Nick Merrick
© Hedrich Blessing

7

.10 restrain

Clark County Government Center
Las Vegas, NV, USA

Fentress Architects
+ Domingo Cambeiro Corporation

Photo: Timothy Hursley

Clark County Government Center
Las Vegas, NV, USA

Fentress Architects
+ Domingo Cambeiro Corporation

Photo: Jeff Goldberg / Esto

.11 restrain

Clark County Government Center
Las Vegas, NV, USA

Fentress Architects
+ Domingo Cambeiro Corporation

Photo: Jeff Goldberg / Esto

Clark County Government Center
Las Vegas, NV, USA

Fentress Architects
+ Domingo Cambeiro Corporation

Photo: Nick Merrick
© Hedrich Blessing

.12 restrain

Clark County Government Center
Las Vegas, NV, USA

Fentress Architects
+ Domingo Cambeiro Corporation

Photo: Timothy Hursley

.13 restrain

University of Colorado Denver Research 1 [+ 2]
Aurora, CO, USA

Fentress Architects
+ Kling Stubbins

Photo: Ron Johnson

.14 restrain

Watermark Luxury Residences
Denver, CO, USA

Fentress Architects

Photo: Jason A. Knowles
© Fentress Architects

.15 restrain

Watermark Luxury Residences
Denver, CO, USA

Fentress Architects

Photo: Jason Jung / Estetico

.16 restrain

International Museum Design Competition

Fentress Architects

© 2009 Fentress Architects

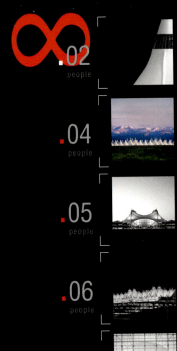

.02 people

Denver International Airport Passenger Terminal Complex
Denver, CO, USA

Fentress Architects
+ Pouw & Associates
+ Bertram A. Bruton & Associates

Photo: Nick Merrick
© Hedrich Blessing

.04 people

Denver International Airport Passenger Terminal Complex
Denver, CO, USA

Fentress Architects
+ Pouw & Associates
+ Bertram A. Bruton & Associates

Photo: © Ellen Jaskol

.05 people

Denver International Airport Passenger Terminal Complex
Denver, CO, USA

Fentress Architects
+ Pouw & Associates
+ Bertram A. Bruton & Associates

Photo: Timothy Hursley

.06 people

Denver International Airport Passenger Terminal Complex
Denver, CO, USA

Fentress Architects
+ Pouw & Associates
+ Bertram A. Bruton & Associates

Photo: Timothy Hursley

.07 people

Denver International Airport Passenger Terminal Complex
Denver, CO, USA

Fentress Architects
+ Pouw & Associates
+ Bertram A. Bruton & Associates

Photo: Timothy Hursley

.08 people

Denver International Airport Passenger Terminal Complex
Denver, CO, USA

Fentress Architects
+ Pouw & Associates
+ Bertram A. Bruton & Associates

Photo: Timothy Hursley

.09 people

Denver International Airport Passenger Terminal Complex
Denver, CO, USA

Fentress Architects
+ Pouw & Associates
+ Bertram A. Bruton & Associates

Photo: Nick Merrick
© Hedrich Blessing

.10 people

Jefferson County Government Center
Golden, CO, USA

Fentress Architects

Photo: Willie Gibson

.11 people

Palazzo Verdi Mixed-Use
Greenwood Village, CO, USA

Fentress Architects

Photo: © Ken Paul

Palazzo Verdi Mixed-Use
Greenwood Village, CO, USA

Fentress Architects

Photo: © Ken Paul

.12 people

One DTC Office Building
Englewood, CO, USA

Fentress Architects

Photo: © Ken Paul

.13 people

Clark County Government Center
Las Vegas, NV, USA

Fentress Architects
+ Domingo Cambeiro Corporation

Photo: Nick Merrick
© Hedrich Blessing

.14 people

Clark County Government Center
Las Vegas, NV, USA

Fentress Architects
+ Domingo Cambeiro Corporation

Photo: Timothy Hursley

Clark County Government Center
Las Vegas, NV, USA

Fentress Architects
+ Domingo Cambeiro Corporation

Photo: Nick Merrick
© Hedrich Blessing

.15 people

California Department of Education Headquarters
Sacramento, CA, USA

Fentress Architects
Design Architect: Johnson Fain

Photo: © Erhard Pfeiffer

.16 people

Colorado State Capitol Life Safety Upgrades + Renovation Phases 1-5
Denver, CO, USA

Fentress Architects

Colorado State Capitol Life Safety Upgrades + Renovation Phases 1-5
Denver, CO, USA

Fentress Architects

Photo: Jason A. Knowles
© Fentress Architects

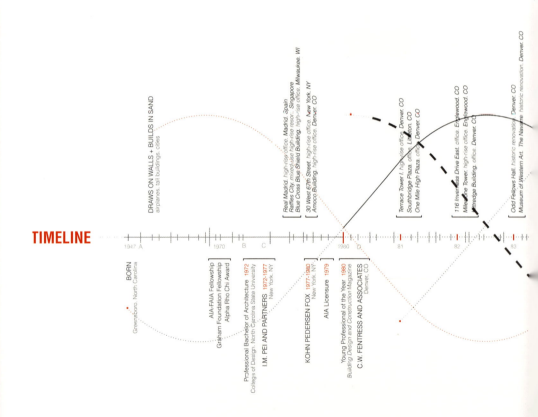

TIMELINE

DRAWS ON WALLS + BUILDS IN SAND
airplanes, tall buildings, cities

Real Madrid, high-rise office. Madrid, Spain
Raffles City, mixed-use high-rise resort. Singapore
Blue Cross Blue Shield Building, high-rise office. Milwaukee, WI
30 West 67th Street, high-rise office. New York, NY
Amoco Building, high-rise office. Denver, CO

Terrace Tower I, high-rise office. Denver, CO
Southbridge Plaza, office. Littleton, CO
One Mile High Plaza, office. Denver, CO

116 Inverness Drive East, office. Englewood, CO
Mile One Tower, high-rise office. Englewood, CO
Ptarmigan Building, office. Denver, CO

Odd Fellows Hall, historic renovation. Denver, CO
Museum of Western Art, The Navarre historic renovation. Denver, CO

1947 A | 1970 B C | 1980 | 81 | 82 | 83

BORN
Greensboro, North Carolina

AIA-FAIA Fellowship
Graham Foundation Fellowship
Alpha Rho Chi Award

Professional Bachelor of Architecture 1972
College of Design, North Carolina State University

I.M. PEI AND PARTNERS 1972-1977
New York, NY

KOHN PEDERSEN FOX 1977-1980
New York, NY

AIA Licensure 1979

Young Professional of the Year 1980
Building Design and Construction Magazine

C.W. FENTRESS AND ASSOCIATES
Denver, CO

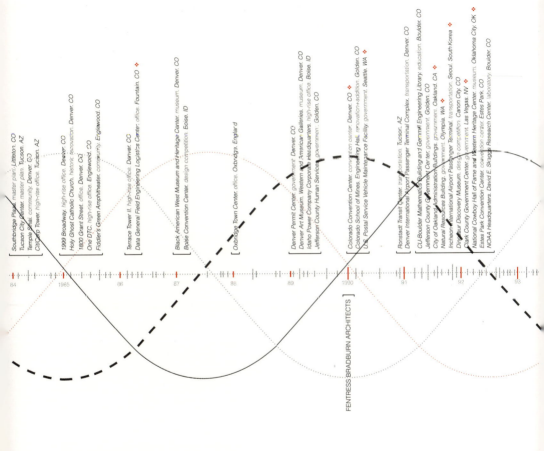

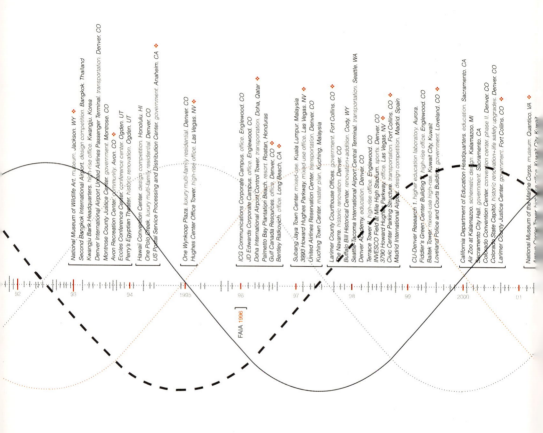

- National Museum of Wildlife Art. *museum.* Jackson, WY ❖
- Second Bangkok International Airport. *design competition.* Bangkok, Thailand
- Kwangju Bank Headquarters. *high-rise office.* Kwangju, Korea
- Denver International Airport United Airlines Passenger Terminal. *transportation.* Denver, CO
- Montrose County Justice Center. *government.* Montrose, CO
- Avon Recreation Center. *community.* Avon, CO ❖
- Eccles Conference Center. *conference center.* Ogden, UT
- Perry's Egyptian Theater. *historic renovation.* Ogden, UT
- Hawaii Convention Center. *design competition.* Honolulu, HI
- One Polo Creek. *luxury multi-family residential.* Denver, CO
- US Postal Service Processing and Distribution Center. *government.* Anaheim, CA ❖

- One Wynkoop Plaza. *luxury multi-family residential.* Denver, CO ❖
- Hughes Center Office Tower. *high-rise office.* Las Vegas, NV ❖

- ICG Communications Corporate Campus. *office.* Englewood, CO
- JD Edwards Corporate Campus. *office.* Englewood, CO
- Doha International Airport Control Tower. *transportation.* Doha, Qatar
- Palmetto Bay Plantation Beach. *resort.* Roatan, Honduras
- Gulf Canada Resources. *office.* Denver, CO ❖
- Bentley Ratkovich. *office.* Long Beach, CA ❖

- Subang Jaya Town Center. *mixed-use.* Kuala Lumpur, Malaysia
- 3903 Howard Hughes Parkway. *mixed-use office.* Las Vegas, NV
- United Airlines Reservation Center. *transportation.* Denver, CO
- Kuching Town Center. *master plan.* Kuching, Malaysia

- Larimer County Courthouse Offices. *government.* Fort Collins, CO
- Le Navarre. *historic renovation.* Denver, CO
- Buffalo Bill Historical Center. *renovation+addition.* Cody, WY
- Seattle-Tacoma International Airport Central Terminal. *transportation.* Seattle, WA
- Denver Academy. *education.* Denver, CO
- Terrace Tower. *high-rise office.* Englewood, CO
- INVESCO Field at Mile High Stadium. *sports.* Denver, CO
- 3790 Howard Hughes Parkway. *office.* Las Vegas, NV ❖
- Civic Center Parking Structure. *transportation.* Fort Collins, CO
- Madrid International Airport. *design competition.* Madrid, Spain

- CU–Denver Research 1. *higher education laboratory.* Aurora
- Fiddler's Green Center Building. *high-rise office.* Englewood, CO
- Baitek Tower. *mixed-use high-rise.* Kuwait City, Kuwait
- Loveland Police and Courts Building. *government.* Loveland, CO

- California Department of Education Headquarters. *education.* Sacramento, CA
- Air Zoo at Kalamazoo. *schematic design.* Kalamazoo, MI
- Sacramento City Hall. *government.* Sacramento, CA
- Colorado Convention Center. *convention center: phase II.* Denver, CO
- Colorado State Capitol. *historic renovation+life safety upgrades.* Denver, CO
- Larimer County Justice Center. *government.* Fort Collins, CO ❖

- National Museum of the Marine Corps. *museum.* Quantico, VA

FAIA 1996

92 · 93 · 94 · 1995 · 96 · 97 · 98 · 99 · 2000 · 01

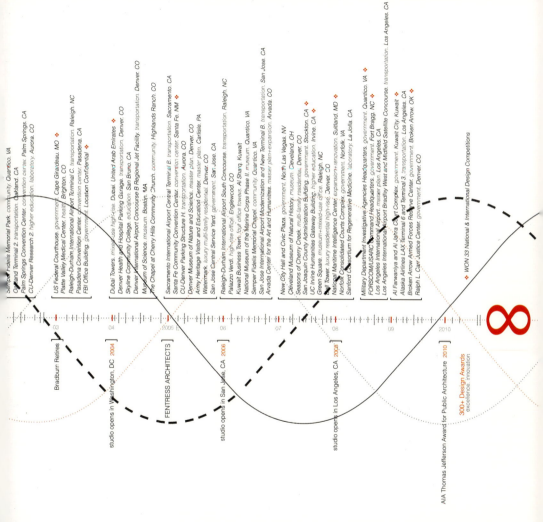

Every effort has been made to trace the original source of copyright material contained in this book. The publishers would be pleased to hear from copyright holders to rectify any errors or omissions.

The information and illustrations in this publication have been prepared and supplied by Fentress Architects. While all reasonable efforts have been made to ensure accuracy, the publishers do not, under any circumstances, accept responsibility for errors, omissions and representations express or implied.